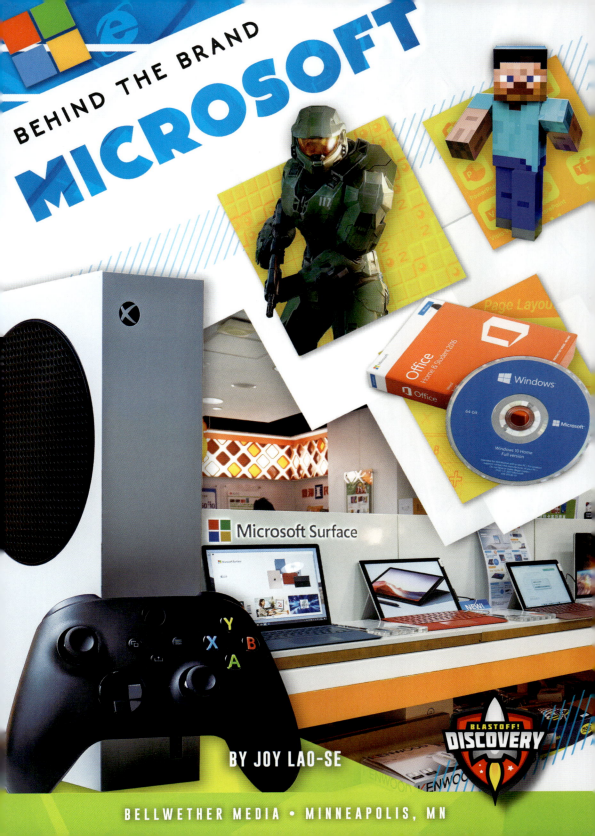

BEHIND THE BRAND
MICROSOFT

BY JOY LAO-SE

BELLWETHER MEDIA • MINNEAPOLIS, MN

This is not an official Microsoft book. It is not approved by or connected with Microsoft Corporation.

This edition first published in 2025 by Bellwether Media, Inc.

No part of this publication may be reproduced in whole or in part without written permission of the publisher.
For information regarding permission, write to Bellwether Media, Inc., Attention: Permissions Department,
6012 Blue Circle Drive, Minnetonka, MN 55343.

Library of Congress Cataloging-in-Publication Data

Names: Lao-se, Joy, author.
Title: Microsoft / by Joy Lao-se.
Description: Minneapolis : Bellwether Media, Inc., [2025] | Series: Blastoff! Discovery : Behind the brand | Includes bibliographical references and index. | Audience: Ages 7-13 | Audience: Grades 4-6 | Summary: "Engaging images accompany information about Microsoft. The combination of high-interest subject matter and narrative text is intended for students in grades 3 through 8"–Provided by publisher.
Identifiers: LCCN 2024046800 (print) | LCCN 2024046801 (ebook) | ISBN 9798893042573 (library binding) | ISBN 9798893044096 (paperback) | ISBN 9798893043549 (ebook)
Subjects: LCSH: Microsoft Corporation–History–Juvenile literature. | Computer software industry–United States–History–Juvenile literature.
Classification: LCC HD9696.63.U64 M53639 2025 (print) | LCC HD9696.63.U64 (ebook) | DDC 338.7/610040973–dc23/eng/20241004
LC record available at https://lccn.loc.gov/2024046800
LC ebook record available at https://lccn.loc.gov/2024046801

Text copyright © 2025 by Bellwether Media, Inc. BLASTOFF! DISCOVERY and associated logos are trademarks and/or registered trademarks of Bellwether Media, Inc.

Editor: Betsy Rathburn   Series Designer: Andrea Schneider   Book Designer: Josh Brink

Printed in the United States of America, North Mankato, MN.

TABLE OF CONTENTS

WORK AND PLAY	4
BOOTING UP	6
NEW UPDATES	18
MICROSOFT MAKES CHANGE	26
FAN FUN	28
GLOSSARY	30
TO LEARN MORE	31
INDEX	32

WORK AND PLAY

A boy powers on his family's Windows computer. He has a paper due tomorrow. He gets out his notes and starts writing in Microsoft Word. He prints his paper when it is done. Then, he starts working on a PowerPoint presentation. He logs off when he finishes his project.

Now, he can play games on his Xbox. He digs through his games to find *Minecraft*. He fights monsters and builds until bedtime. Microsoft products helped him do work and have fun!

POWERPOINT APP

MINECRAFT

BOOTING UP

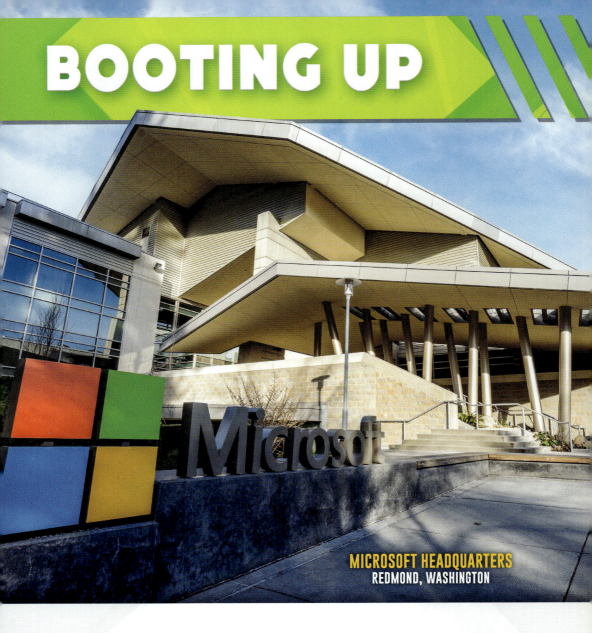

MICROSOFT HEADQUARTERS
REDMOND, WASHINGTON

Microsoft is a technology company known for its **software**. The Windows **operating system** (OS) is the most famous. Microsoft also makes **hardware** like computers and gaming **consoles**. Its **headquarters** is in Redmond, Washington.

Microsoft Word, PowerPoint, and Excel are **apps** that help people run businesses and do schoolwork. People use the Microsoft Surface **tablet** to work or use the internet. LinkedIn helps job seekers find work. Gamers can use the Xbox to play their favorite video games. Microsoft offers useful products for everyone!

MICROSOFT HEADQUARTERS

REDMOND, WASHINGTON

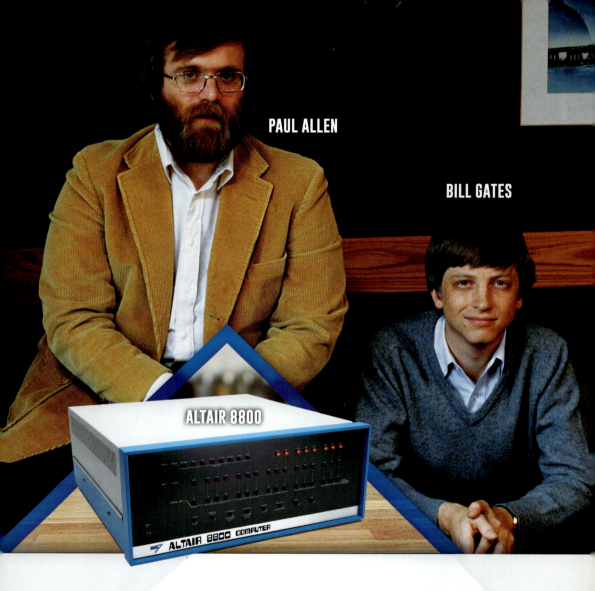

Microsoft was **founded** by Bill Gates and Paul Allen on April 4, 1975. The Altair 8800 was a new personal computer made by a company called MITS. Bill and Paul created a new version of a **programming language** that would work with the Altair. They sold it to MITS. It became known as Altair BASIC.

This success led Bill and Paul to form their own company. They chose the name Microsoft. It was a combination of the words "microprocessor" and "software." They quickly started to grow their new company.

BILL GATES

BORN October 28, 1955, in Seattle, Washington

ROLE Cofounder and former leader of Microsoft

ACCOMPLISHMENTS

Grew Microsoft into the biggest technology company in the world

In 1980, Microsoft made a deal with a company called IBM. Microsoft would create the OS for IBM's first personal computer. The OS was called MS-DOS. It was released in 1981. It became important software for all personal computers. It helped Microsoft earn money and grow.

EARLY IBM PERSONAL COMPUTER

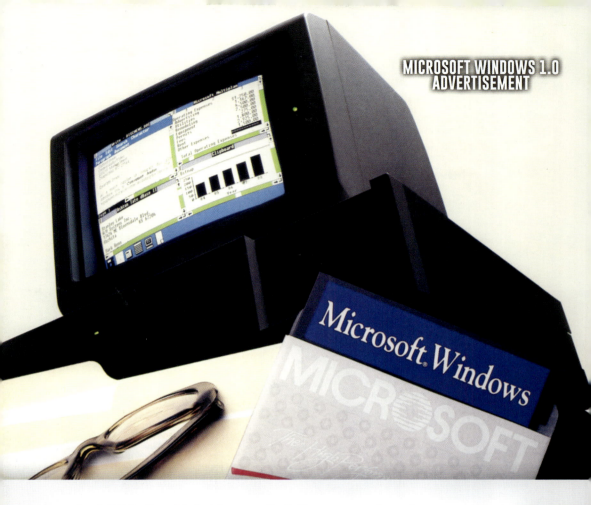

MICROSOFT WINDOWS 1.0 ADVERTISEMENT

In 1983, Paul left Microsoft. Bill continued as the company's leader. By 1985, Microsoft had released Windows 1.0. It was Microsoft's first **graphical user interface** (GUI). Instead of typing commands, users could click with a mouse. They could also run multiple apps at once. It was the first Microsoft OS to include apps like Notepad and Calculator.

NEW NAME

Windows 1.0 also had a painting app. It is now known as Microsoft Paint!

Microsoft Office was released for Apple's Mac OS in 1989. A year later, it was released on Windows. It included Word, PowerPoint, Excel, and Mail. These apps helped people get work done. By the end of 1990, Microsoft had over 5,000 employees. Sales had reached over $1 billion!

EARLY MICROSOFT PRODUCTS

1981 MS-DOS

1982 MICROSOFT FLIGHT SIMULATOR

1985 WINDOWS 1.0

1985 MICROSOFT PAINT

1987 MICROSOFT WORKS

Microsoft's *Encarta* was launched in 1993. Users bought a program to use with their computers. This let them look up different topics. They could find text, pictures, and more. Later, *Encarta* was available on the internet. It lasted until 2009!

13

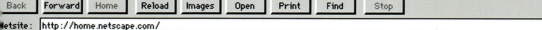

By the 1990s, the internet was growing quickly. In 1994, Netscape Navigator was released. This **browser** made using the internet easy. It was very popular. But users had to pay for it.

In 1995, Microsoft released its own browser called Internet Explorer (IE). It eventually came free with Windows computers. This made Netscape less popular. Microsoft was accused of breaking an **antitrust law**. Some thought it was stopping people from using its competitors' products. Microsoft was fined for its practices. But IE continued as the most popular browser.

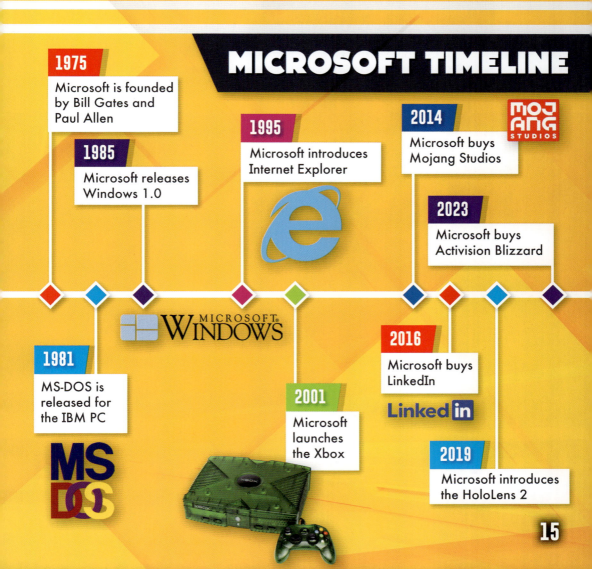

MICROSOFT TIMELINE

1975 — Microsoft is founded by Bill Gates and Paul Allen

1981 — MS-DOS is released for the IBM PC

1985 — Microsoft releases Windows 1.0

1995 — Microsoft introduces Internet Explorer

2001 — Microsoft launches the Xbox

2014 — Microsoft buys Mojang Studios

2016 — Microsoft buys LinkedIn

2019 — Microsoft introduces the HoloLens 2

2023 — Microsoft buys Activision Blizzard

Microsoft continued to update Windows. Windows 95 was known for being user-friendly. It was the first version to have a Start menu! In 2001, Microsoft released Windows XP. This OS had a smoother performance. Users could **customize** the look. Many people and businesses used it!

FLYING HIGH

Microsoft Flight Simulator was first released in 1982. This game lets players practice flying an airplane. It is one of the longest-running computer games ever!

WINDOWS XP PACKAGING

WINDOWS 95 EVENT

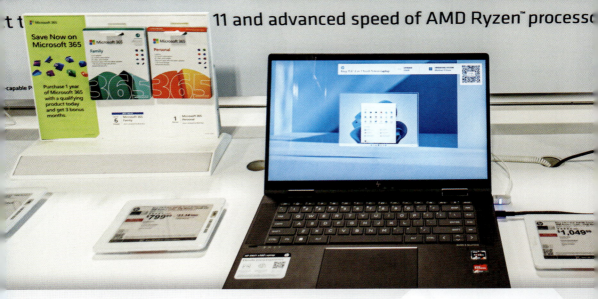

Many new versions of Windows followed. Windows 7 came out in 2009. It was faster than previous versions. Users could organize apps and windows more easily. In 2021, Windows 11 was released. Many of its new features were great for gamers. Games loaded quickly. **Graphics** were more detailed. New versions of Windows will continue to improve the OS!

NEW UPDATES

MASTER CHIEF

Microsoft also began releasing new hardware. In 2001, it released the Xbox console. More than 24 million original Xboxes sold! The console released with many new games. *Halo: Combat Evolved* was among the most popular. Players control a character named Master Chief. They explore space and fight aliens. The game became one of the best-selling games **exclusive** to Xbox consoles.

Mad Dash Racing was another Xbox game released in 2001. Players choose characters and race around different tracks. *Arctic Thunder* was another popular racing game. Players race on snowmobiles!

ON TV, TOO!

In 2022, a TV series based on Halo video games began. But it was canceled after two seasons.

XBOX 360 DISPLAY

HALO 4

Microsoft continued to release new versions of the Xbox. The Xbox 360 was released in 2005. It was the best-selling Xbox ever. More than 84 million sold! Many popular games released on this console. The Halo series continued with *Halo 3* in 2007 and *Halo 4* in 2012.

In 2013, the Xbox One was released. This console brought more power to the Xbox. New controllers also improved the gaming experience. In 2020, the Xbox Series S and Series X were released. The Series S was all **digital**. The Series X was the most powerful Xbox yet. It ran faster and had more storage for games!

XBOX VERSIONS

XBOX
Released: 2001

XBOX 360
Released: 2005

XBOX ONE
Released: 2013

XBOX SERIES X
Released: 2020

XBOX SERIES S
Released: 2020

Microsoft-owned **studios** make games for Xbox and Windows computers. These include the Forza series. This series lets players race cars. *Grounded* is another game by a Microsoft studio. Players control ant-sized characters in a backyard.

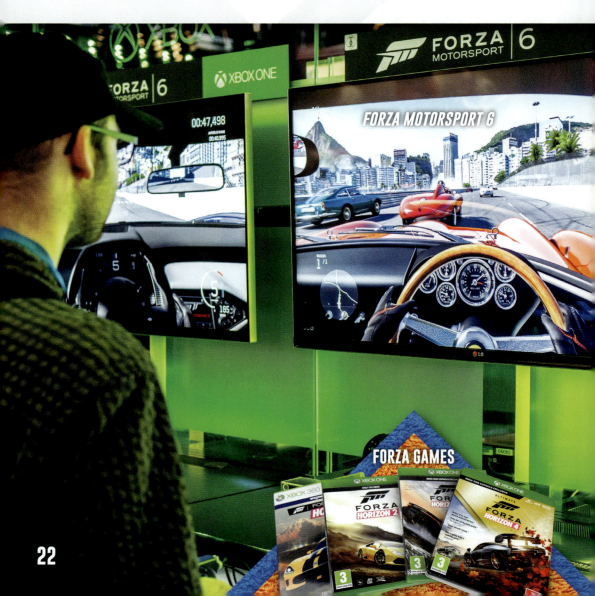

In 2014, Microsoft bought Mojang Studios. This meant that Microsoft now owned *Minecraft*. The game changed and grew. More items and monsters were added. In 2023, Microsoft bought Activision Blizzard. This gave Microsoft control of many more popular games. These include the Overwatch and Crash Bandicoot series. Microsoft fans will never run out of fun games to play!

SURFACE GO 2

HOLOLENS

Microsoft

Microsoft has added other hardware, too. In 2012, it released the first Surface tablet. It had a touchscreen and a keyboard like a laptop. But the device did not sell well. Microsoft lost $900 million. Still, Microsoft released improved Surface models. Sales grew. In 2022, the Surface line earned $6.7 billion!

In 2015, Microsoft released the HoloLens. This headset projects images onto the real world. In 2019, the improved HoloLens 2 came out. The U.S. Army bought around 10,000 special versions of the headset called IVAS. IVAS headsets help soldiers use maps and fly **drones**. Microsoft continues to release exciting new games and hardware!

MICROSOFT EARNINGS

- $3.75 BILLION IN 1993
- $32.19 BILLION IN 2003
- $77.85 BILLION IN 2013
- $211.92 BILLION IN 2020

MICROSOFT MAKES CHANGE

TEAM RUBICON

Microsoft gives money to help others. Since 2018, it has given $5 million to Team Rubicon to help after disasters. It also gives money to help the earth. It has **invested** $1 billion to create technology that could be used to slow **climate change**.

Microsoft also helps people access technology. The TEALS Program started in 2009. It has helped over 100,000 students learn about computer science. The IT Makeover Campaign helps **nonprofit** organizations get technology. Microsoft has given more than $300,000 to more than 45 nonprofits through this program!

GIVING BACK

$5 MILLION
GIVEN TO TEAM RUBICON SINCE 2018

$1 BILLION
INVESTED TO CREATE TECHNOLOGY TO SLOW CLIMATE CHANGE

100,000
STUDENTS REACHED BY TEALS PROGRAM SINCE 2009

$300,000
GIVEN TO PROVIDE TECHNOLOGY FOR NONPROFITS THROUGH IT MAKEOVER CAMPAIGN

FAN FUN

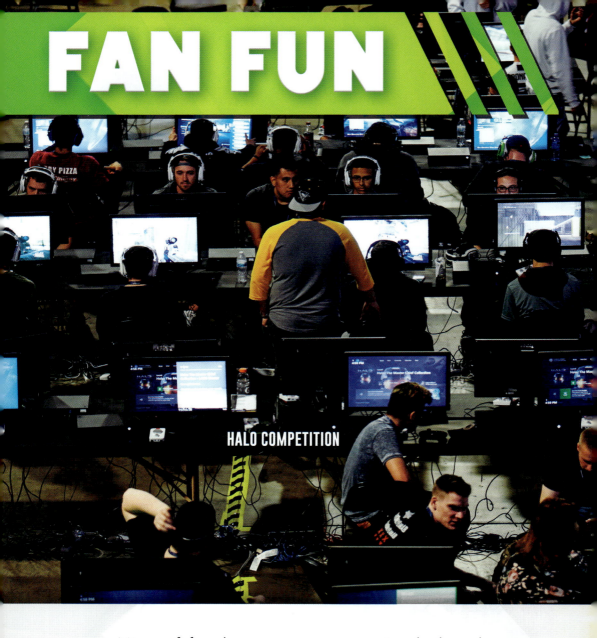

HALO COMPETITION

Microsoft fans have many ways to enjoy the brand. Gamers can learn about exciting news through events like the Xbox Games Showcase. This event is streamed online. The company shares updates and shows off new products and games. In 2024, the company announced new Xbox consoles!

Fans also connect with each other through Xbox FanFest. This online club tells fans about events and contests they might enjoy. Competitions are common among Xbox and computer gamers. Halo and Forza competitions are popular. Microsoft and Xbox have many fans all around the world!

XBOX GAMES SHOWCASE

WHAT IT IS

An online stream where new Xbox games and consoles are introduced

WHEN IT HAPPENS

Once every year

WHERE IT HAPPENS

Online

GLOSSARY

antitrust law—a law that stops companies from using unfair business practices

apps—programs such as games or an internet browser; apps are also called applications.

browser—a program used to access the World Wide Web

climate change—a human-caused change in Earth's weather due to warming temperatures

consoles—electronic devices mainly used for playing video games

customize—to make or change something to fit a user's needs

digital—related to electronic or computer technology

drones—aircraft that are flown by a remote control or by computers

exclusive—not available on other consoles

founded—started or created

graphical user interface—a computer system that allows a user to control a computer by clicking icons and windows using a mouse

graphics—art such as illustrations or designs

hardware—parts of a computer that people can touch

headquarters—a company's main office

invested—put money into a project in hopes of earning more money later

nonprofit—not operating to make money for its owner

operating system—computer software that allows programs to run

programming language—a system of coding for computers

software—computer programs that do specific tasks

studios—places where video games are made

tablet—a type of computer that has thin hardware and is easy to move

TO LEARN MORE

AT THE LIBRARY

Goldstein, Margaret J. *The Genius of Microsoft: How Bill Gates and Windows Changed the World.* Minneapolis, Minn.: Lerner Publications, 2022.

Green, Sara. *Apple*. Minneapolis, Minn.: Bellwether Media, 2024.

Noll, Elizabeth. *Computer Programmer*. Minneapolis, Minn.: Bellwether Media, 2023.

ON THE WEB

FACTSURFER

Factsurfer.com gives you a safe, fun way to find more information.

1. Go to www.factsurfer.com.

2. Enter "Microsoft" into the search box and click 🔍.

3. Select your book cover to see a list of related content.

INDEX

Allen, Paul, 8, 9, 11
Altair BASIC, 8
antitrust law, 14, 15
apps, 5, 7, 11, 12, 17
computers, 5, 6, 8, 10, 13, 15, 16, 22, 29
early Microsoft products, 12
Encarta, 13
fans, 23, 28, 29
Forza (series), 22, 29
Gates, Bill, 8, 9, 11, 14
giving back, 27
Halo (series), 18, 19, 20, 28, 29
HoloLens, 25
Internet Explorer, 15
IT Makeover Campaign, 27
Microsoft earnings, 25
Microsoft Flight Simulator, 16
Microsoft Office, 5, 7, 12
Microsoft Surface, 7, 24
Minecraft, 5, 23
MS-DOS, 10
name, 9
Netscape Navigator, 14, 15
Redmond, Washington, 6, 7
sales, 12, 18, 20, 24, 25
studios, 22, 23
TEALS Program, 27
Team Rubicon, 26
timeline, 15
video games, 5, 7, 16, 17, 18, 19, 20, 21, 22, 23, 25, 28, 29
Windows, 5, 6, 11, 12, 13, 15, 16, 17, 22
Xbox, 5, 7, 18, 19, 20, 21, 22, 28, 29
Xbox Games Showcase, 28, 29
Xbox versions, 21

The images in this book are reproduced through the courtesy of: Mr.Mikla, front cover (Xbox Series S), p. 24 (Surface Go 2); Sorbis, front cover (Microsoft Surface); Nor Gal, front cover (Microsoft Office); PixieMe, front cover (Excel spreadsheet); Miguel Lagoa, front cover (*Halo Infinity*), pp. 16 (*Microsoft Flight Simulator*), 25 (Xbox Series X); tomeqs, front cover (*Minesweeper*); Pabkov, front cover (*Minecraft*); Koshiro K, front cover (Microsoft apps); Poetra.RH, front cover (Microsoft logo); monticello, front cover (Internet Explorer icon), p. 9 (laptop); MMXeon, p. 2; Pieter Beens, pp. 3, 27 (bottom right); Phynart Studio, pp. 4-5; Mikhail Primakov, p. 5 (PowerPoint); dpa/ Alamy, pp. 5 (*Minecraft*), 10 (Bill Gates); Tada Images, p. 6 (headquarters); Ian Dewar Photography, p. 7 (Redmond, Washington); Doug Wilson/ Getty Images, p. 8 (Bill Gates and Paul Allen); Mark Madeo/ Future/ Getty Images, p. 8 (Altair 8800); Terrence Mayes/ Alamy, p. 10 (early IBM personal computer); Microsoft/ Swtpc6800/ Wikipedia, pp. 11 (Windows 1.0 advertisement), 15 (Windows 1.0); Microsoft Corporation/ Wikipedia, pp. 11 (Microsoft Paint icon), 15 (MS-DOS logo), 23 (MS-DOS logo); srwitmer77/ eBay, p. 12 (Microsoft Paint); DatBot/ Wikipedia, p. 12 (*Microsoft Flight Simulator*); sircattywompus/ The House of Wompus/ eBay, p. 12 (Microsoft Works); Patti McConville/ Alamy, p. 13 (*Encarta* advertisement); Christina Leaf, p. 13 (*Encarta* disc); Darklanlan/ Wikipedia, p. 13 (Windows characters); AP Photo/ AP Newsroom, p. 14 (Netscape Navigator); Douglas Graham/ Getty Images, p. 14 (Bill Gates); Pivotman319/ Wikipedia, p. 15 (Internet Explorer logo); robtek, p. 15 (Xbox); Diego Thomazini, p. 15 (LinkedIn); sdx15, p. 16 (*Microsoft Flight Simulator*); Konektus Photo, p. 16 (Windows XP packaging); DB/ picture-alliance/ dpa/ AP Images/ AP Newroom, p. 16 (Windows 95 event); Jeff Greenberg/ Getty Images, p. 17 (Windows 11 laptop display); Kim Kulish/ Corbis/ Getty Images, p. 18 (Master Chief); AaronP/ Bauer-Griffin/ GC Images/ Getty Images, p. 19 (Halo TV series); julie deshaies, pp. 19 (Xbox, Xbox controller), 21 (Xbox); manjim-4153/ The Forgotten Locker/ eBay, p. 19 (*Arctic Thunder*); Nick's Fantastic Finds/ eBay, p. 19 (*Mad Dash Racing*); Koichi Kamoshida/ Getty Images, p. 20 (Xbox 360 display); razorpix/ Alamy, p. 20 (*Halo 4*); CaptNorth, p. 21 (Xbox 360); Miguel Angel Bistrain, p. 21 (Xbox One); Jim1982, p. 21 (Xbox Series X); Jair Fonseca, p. 21 (Xbox Series S); Sergey Galyonkin/ Wikipedia, p. 22 (*Forza Motorsport 6*); SJBright/ Alamy, p. 22 (Forza games); Rocklights/ Stockimo/ Alamy, p. 23 (*Minecraft*); Rokas Tenys/ Alamy, p. 23 (*Overwatch 2*); Chesnot/ Getty Images, p. 24 (HoloLens); Lightspruch, p. 25 (Xbox); Sergei Elagin, p. 25 (Activision Blizzard); Miguel Lagoa, p. 25 (Xbox Series X); Operation 2024/ Alamy, p. 26 (Team Rubicon); ElenaR, p. 27 (top left); Gorodenkoff, p. 27 (top right); Monkey Business Images, p. 27 (bottom left); Cooper Neill / Stringer/ Getty Images, p. 28 (Halo competition); Casey Rodgers/ AP Images, p. 29 (Xbox Games Showcase); urbanbuzz, p. 31 (*Minecraft*); Jack Skeens, p. 31 (Microsoft Surface Duo).